Omega Psi Phi Ultimate Uplift:

1911 to 2011 and Beyond!

By Marzette Henderson Jr.

Email: mhendersonjr32@yahoo.com

Website; mhendersonjr.com

Published by: Hyde Park Publishing.

Editor: Ayana Trice-Henderson
Designer: Nelson Grant (ΑΦΑ)

ISBN: 978-0-578-08790-0

Acknowledgments:

I give infinite gratitude to God for being the channel/vessel for Omega Psi Phi Ultimate Uplift. Also, I would like to give infinite gratitude to my beautiful wife Ayana Eliza Trice-Henderson for all your unconditional love, help, and understanding during my mission to make positive changes in Omega Psi Phi and the World; you are the great love of my life and have been very instrumental and dedicated in supporting me on my mission of uplift. I would also like to give the most deep thanks to my family that breathed life into me including my mother Jacqueline Kay Henderson; Mom, you are not here to see I am a Que, I will work to honor your memory and to where you would be proud of me; I will work for both of us. Also my father Marzette Henderson Sr. as well as Cleotha Moss Sr., Nathaniel and Juanita Bryant, Rosie Lee Boyd and Robert White, Maua Henderson, Casarine Davis, Lawrence Moss. I give the deepest gratitude to **The Most Honorable Dr. Ernest Everett Just, The Most Honorable Bishop Edgar Amos Love, The Most Honorable Dr. Oscar James Cooper,** and **The Most Honorable Professor Frank Coleman,** also known as the **Ques,** for giving life to **Omega Psi Phi Fraternity Incorporated** and the divine principles of **Manhood, Scholarship, Perseverance,** and **Uplift.** I would also like to give deep gratitude to **Epsilon Beta Chapter** -- the Uplift chapter, including the *following brothers: William Lucky, Leonardo Jones, Sterling Gant, Byron Williams, Terry Robinson, Cydney Muhammad, David Green, Jefferson Davis, Roy Shephard, Troy Collins, Virgil Huff, Erick Smith Sr., David Yarborough, Jabril Muhammad, Andre Small, Darrek Bramlett, Oscar Scott, Rah Ama, Allatwon Jackson, Kendall Moore, Steven Tinch, David Kenebrew, Michael Thornton Jr., and the thousands of brothers I have met that have positively affected my life including: Dr. William A. Smith, Estavon Hampton, Alphrin Norman, and Fredrick Brown. Also the Ques and everyone that will uplift the Ques through this medium: Abdel K. Muhammad, Andre Kipatrick, Andre marshall, Anthony Kelly, Anton White, Antwan Taylor, Baron Weston, Bomani Sundai, Carl A. Blunt, Calvin Attoh, Climent Edmond, C. Tyrone Gilmore, Dave Allsbrook, David Barnes, David Lee, D. Michael Lyles, Jr., Fredrick Banks, Frederick Johnson, Fredrick P. Williams, Gary L. Flowers, Gilbert V. Richardson, Hank Beatty, Harold H. Webb, Herbert Tucker, Jacques Miles James Peters, James Thomas, Jay Poindexter, Jean Claude Aurel, Jeffrey Carter. Jeff Mckamey, Johnny Lynch, Johnny Watters, Hank Beatty, Harold W. Webb, Jeff Mc Kamey, Ron L. Blanch, Sloan Touissant Baptiste, Steven Millner, Terence Hamilton, Terry Pickens. Terry Robinson. Tre Hodge, Troy Collins, Walter H. Maczyk, William H. Harris, and William Lucky. Also Id like to give love to our special guests Madonna C.Jackson and Tanneka Howard.*

Dedication:

I AM dedicating this book to God, our Founders, and the uplift of Omega Psi Phi.

Introduction:

The Founders were on a mission. The three young Howard university undergraduate students received the inspiration to birth Omega Psi Phi. Edgar Amos Love, Oscar James Cooper, and Frank Coleman, took their vision to their faculty adviser Professor Ernest Everett Just. All four combined their love, peace, and happiness and Omega Psi Phi was born. Omega Psi Phi means "Friendship Is Essential To The Soul;" Manhood, Scholarship, Perseverance, and Uplift manifested as the cardinal principles. The Founding Fathers "knew" Omega Psi phi would live forever; they laid the foundation to insure we have what we need in order to do so. The Founders graduated and went on to distinguished careers in their chosen professions: Bishop Edgar Amos Love went on to be the Bishop of the United Methodist Church; Dr. Oscar James Cooper became a prominent doctor with a practice in Philadelphia that flourished for over 50 years; Professor Frank Coleman stayed working and building Omega Psi Phi from the Mother Pearl, becoming a professor immediately and later the Chairman of the Department of Physics at Howard University; and Dr. Ernest Everett Just became the first world famous African American biologist. When Omega Psi Phi was established, Howard Universities President did not want to recognize the brotherhood as a national organization. Brothers of

1

Omega Psi Phi persevered until they achieved national recognition for our organization and now we are international and strong. Now, there have been over 940 plus chapters of Omega Psi Phi chartered throughout the United States, Bermuda, Bahamas, Canada, Germany, Japan, Korea, Kuwait, Liberia, and the Virgin Islands. There are many notable Omega Men recognized as leaders in academics, the arts, business, civil rights, education, government, sports, and the sciences sectors at the local, national and international level. The Ques have worked and prayed to create an infinitely powerful force of men dedicated to the Cardinal Principles of Manhood, Scholarship, Perseverance, and Uplift. Manhood, which is character, a Que is a man of sterling worth with unsullied character. Scholarship, the Ques intellectual ability is above average. Perseverance, a Que can accomplish any dream or goal and overcome any obstacle or challenge. Uplift, the Ques stay steadfast to the purpose of uplifting humanity. Omega Psi Phi continues to be highly successful because our Founders Love, Cooper, Coleman, and Just were men of the very highest spirits and intelligence. The Founders selected and attracted men of similar ideals and characteristics. There is no accident that many of America's great African American leaders are/were Omega Men. Since the beginning, Omega Psi Phi has touched millions of lives in a positive *manner. Omega Psi Phi has a very dynamic heritage that is to be protected, honored, celebrated, and expanded!*

*Omega Psi Phi Ultimate UPLIFT; 1911 to 2011 and Beyond! is a **Bold Action** to cause a positive difference in Omega Psi Phi and the consciousness of the Ques. In 1996, I was told <u>America will change, when the Ques change</u> by Br. Dr. William A. Smith, 84- Tau Theta- Eastern Illinois University. At the time he was a Professor at Western Illinois University, where I graduated. We were in the Que House at the time. When he told me this it triggered complete awareness. I mentally searched through all the Ques I currently knew, all the Ques there had been and even the Ques to come. It was a moment of complete awareness. I was thinking who is going to do this, who is going to uplift the Ques? In that same moment I knew he probably never said this to anyone before and probably would never say it again. I knew instantly that if I didn't do it, no one else would. This was my spiritual mission; this was my divine purpose. This was God's Job for me, my very reason for coming into Omega Psi Phi and this World--to uplift the Ques. At the time, I didn't know how I was going to do it but, I did what I needed to do to expand--the result is Omega Psi Phi Ultimate UPLIFT: 1911 to 2011 and Beyond! Omega Psi Phi Ultimate Uplift upholds the responsibilities that all Omegas have pledged and sworn an oath to uphold. Uplift is why we are here in Omega*

3

Psi Phi and the World, this is our divine purpose, this is God's job for us and this book is evidence that we, as the Ques, are helping to make Omega Psi Phi Fraternity Incorporated, America, and the World a better/happier place in which to live. Omega Psi Phi Ultimate UPLIFT is from the Creator, and the Ques, for our uplift. Read it on a continual basis; it is designed to positively change our life in Omega Psi Phi and raise our enthusiastic vibrations. America is self-correcting and the world is positively changing. It will also help you add to your Divine-Que unity, live with unlimited enthusiasm and excitement, express brotherly love and your ideal, add to your Christian Manhood, be our brother's keeper, and help you to believe and know that we are self-correcting and we the Ques, are uplifting America from her place of apostasy towards recognition of her Master; and when America changes, the World will change.

Infinitely Happy Que Year! 2011 is a great year for the Ques, our family, and friends. The Ques have chosen to seek loving brothers, friends, and family and serving Omega Psi Phi Fraternity Incorporated rather than worldly things.

Ω

OMEGA is one!

Ω

The Ques are great, mighty, and powerful.

Ω

God sent the Ques!

Ω

The Ques are a 'Force of One."

Ω

The united chapters of Omega Psi Phi:

Regardless of what chapter or district we are from, we are all united under one Omega Psi Phi Fraternity. Our souls are all one. All the Ques in the Omega Psi Phi Fraternity are united with one another. Regardless of our process, we are all Ques united under one Omega Psi Phi Fraternity and the only law is --"Friendship Is Essential To The Soul." We should treat all the Ques as if they were a part of our soul because they are.

5

Omega Psi Phi has been be blessed from the very beginning, not only by our Founding Fathers, but by the chapters of Ques throughout the world. Thousands of Ques, have worked hard and prayed hard for the success of Omega Psi Phi. OMEGA is now this great created being and we are the part of her that knows she lives. Now, the fate of Omega Psi Phi rests on us and on our abilities, both individually and collectively, to continue to move Omega Psi Phi in the direction in accordance with the Founding Fathers and God's plan. The Ques response to God has been great thus far. As we continue uplifting in the name of Omega Psi Phi, God will continue to bless us to be strong, intelligent, virile, and enthusiastic with the ability to help others improve their living conditions.

Ω

You are a Que, you can do anything positive!

Ω

The Ques can navigate the politics of the fraternity while advancing brotherhood.

Ω

It is tough pledging Que; it is tougher being a Que.

Ω

The Ques are a "force of one" that has been sent to make positive changes for the betterment of black people and humanity and we have been making a real difference.

Humans operate at a relatively low vibration level and human energy is lower in general. There are humans that have higher energy levels though. The Ques have high energy intensity because we have chosen to take the initiative to consciously use Omega Psi Phi to evolve our souls.

Ω

The Ques are serious about Omega Psi Phi Fraternity Incorporated.

Ω

The Ques affect each other because we are all part of each other. The Ques affect all chapters of Omega Psi Phi because all chapters of Omega Psi Phi interweave and interrelate with all other chapters.

Ω

We love the Founding Fathers and always uphold their four cardinal principles. Always remember Ques, the Founding Fathers have blessed us personally and this means for keeps!

Ω

Omega Psi Phi is the means for us attaining our goal of true friendship and the uplift of humanity. The life or death of Omega Psi Phi Incorporated depends on us. As the Ques, our most essential mission is to lead Omega Psi Phi in the correct direction without the slightest misstep. This is what the Ques are for!

7

The Omega Psi Phi Fraternity Incorporated experience is our opportunity, for our souls to advance, towards the ideal of complete friendship with the Ques.

Ω

The Omegas are the Sons of Blood and Thunder and a super-human manifestation of the Creator.

Ω

The Ques are leaders among men, women, and children rather than followers.

Ω

God is within the Ques and the Ques are an inseparable part of God. Omega Psi Phi is perfect as a creation of God. The Ques and God are one and we must love both -- the Creator and Created.

Ω

Treat the Ques as you would like to be treated.

Ω

The Ques stay thoroughly immersed in the True Omega Spirit.

Ω

Always talk to the Ques enthusiastically and with respect.

Neos enthusiastically arise and make your entrance. With a direct connection to the Founding Fathers, achieve overwhelming victory for Omega Psi Phi Fraternity Incorporated. As the youth of the Omega Psi Phi, uplift Black America, America, and the World to its core.

Ω

We should have been very willing, even anxious, as men, to accept pledging Omega Psi Phi in order to help us better ourselves as Ques. Compared to a lifetime as Ques, the time, pain, and the hardship we spent pledging Omega Psi Phi, was insignificant. The difficulty we experienced pledging Omega Psi Phi was for just a moment, just a split second of consciousness, and we should have been very willing to endure it.

Ω

Goddesses find the Ques irresistible and the Ques love and respect Goddesses.

Ω

The Ques are great leaders that tell you how to get where you are going, and even greater leaders that take you there.

Ω

The Ques have a good blend of book knowledge and street knowledge, which makes us dangerous to the darkness and extremely powerful. We can operate on all levels and are comfortable in every environment.

Having a Que as a friend is one of the best things you can have, and being a Que that is a friend to the Ques is one of the best things you can be.

Ω

Omega Psi Phi Fraternity Incorporated is only as strong as each Que. As Ques, we are all linked together. What one Que does affects all the other Ques. This is why it is important to help the Ques. We are not only helping them, we are helping ourselves and Omega Psi Phi Fraternity Incorporated.

Ω

We should love God, the Founders, and Omega Psi Phi Incorporated with all our hearts, our minds, and our bodies and love the Ques and others as we love ourselves.

Ω

For the Ques, enthusiasm is the fuel of our lives. It helps the Ques get to where Omega Psi Phi Fraternity Incorporated needs to go.

Ω

Within the Light of Omega, we realize that everyone and everything is connected to OMEGA. In the Light of Omega is the cure for the disease that has afflicted our community, the knowledge to achieve personal success. The Light of Omega contains wisdom, love, friendship, and enthusiasm beyond all comprehension.

10

Omega Psi Phi is great because the Ques and others have sacrificed our own personal desires for the great cause of Omega Psi Phi Fraternity Incorporated. By doing so we never die, we never disappear. OMEGA is the way we will live on. This is what it means to be a Que!

Ω

Out of many, the Ques are one. No matter what line we were on, we are all joined under one Omega Psi Phi Fraternity Incorporated. All the Ques souls are one and all Ques are protected thought association.

Ω

We are the Que part of Omega Psi Phi Fraternity Incorporated. This is a most fantastic blessing. It is a blessing beyond our wildest imagination of what a blessing can be.

Ω

The Ques are responsible adults that make the right choices.

Ω

Every Que has a definite mission to do in Omega Psi Phi Fraternity Incorporated. We must find and do our mission.

Ω

Our individual thoughts and actions make an impact on Omega Psi Phi Fraternity Incorporated -- the whole.

11

There is only one truly significant work to do in Omega Psi Phi, and that is love; to love the Ques, to love family and friends, to love service, to love Omega herself, just because she exists.

Ω

The Ques are all connected and we know each other. All the Ques are of Omega Psi Phi Fraternity Incorporated.

Ω

"Respect": Omega Psi Phi, the Ritual, the grip, the 4 and 20, by laws, the Ques, the women, the people, the movement, Mother Nature, the system, and thy self.

Ω

The Ques are great men, but are not born great. God uses Omega Psi Phi Fraternity Incorporated to make us great!

Ω

Omega Psi Phi Fraternity Incorporated is a golden opportunity to be a light for the Creator and live a spiritual life, in a world of darkness.

Ω

When we give and share what we have with the Ques and Omega Psi Phi Fraternity Incorporated, we will receive more. This is a Spiritual Law. We will be given all that we are prepared to receive.

12

The Ques are globally linked and this makes each of us a part of one whole Omega Psi Phi. We are all divinely connected with all of Omega Psi Phi Fraternity Incorporated.

Ω

The Ques are very special people with important missions have been placed all over the World so that we might uplift others!

Ω

Talk to the Ques how you want to be talked to.

Ω

The ultimate measure of an Omega Man is not where he stands in moments of joy and celebration, but where he stands in times of service, friendship, and when he is needed.

Ω

A Que is a real friend that will never get away from you, nor try to, nor want to.

Ω

The Founders participated with God in the creation of Omega Psi Phi; which was created for the purpose of our spiritual growth and friendship. They participated in planning the future of Omega Psi Phi, including the Four Cardinal Principals which would govern us and the spiritual power of enthusiasm we would be able to access.

13

A Que is a man of sterling worth with unsullied character.

Ω

The Ques use our abilities to stay steadfast to the purpose of Omega Psi Phi Fraternity Incorporated and the cause of uplifting humanity.

Ω

The Ques intellectual ability is above average.

Ω

The Ques are here to help others attain a higher level mentally, morally, and spiritually, and improve the living conditions of others.

Ω

Do unto the Ques as you would have the Ques do unto you.

Ω

Omega Men have a responsibility and a privilege, of helping to lead America and the World into a better age.

Ω

Omega Psi Phi Fraternity Incorporated stays on the Ques hearts and minds.

If you want to have the Ques as friends, than show yourself to be friendly. If you want to have fun, than make fun for the Ques and friends!

Ω

In order to bring out the best in the Ques and those surrounding us; we should give them encouragement and show them loving appreciation.

Ω

Pledging Omega Psi Phi was difficult. We must not have skipped over the difficult parts. Everyone must earn the Omega Psi Phi Fraternity Incorporated they receive.

Ω

The Ques understand friendship is the most priceless gift that can be given.

Ω

The Ques are your friends that will love you if your wife or girl deserts you.

Ω

The Ques, our families, and friends co-create the Kingdom of Heaven on Earth. Nothing can stop the Ques, our families, and friends from co-creating the Kingdom of Heaven on Earth.

The Ques get down how we live -- enthusiastically.

Ω

Omega Psi Phi Fraternity Incorporated has done great works and continues to do great works.

Ω

God never leaves the Ques alone.

Ω

Pledging was temporary; brotherly love is forever.

Ω

The Ques must look on the positive side of the Omega Psi Phi Fraternity Incorporated experience.

Ω

Omega Psi Phi Fraternity Incorporated is a society full of great men.

Ω

The Ques are meant to show love to every Que we meet and everyone we meet on behalf of Omega Psi Phi Fraternity Incorporated. When we show love we receive and experience a tremendous love from the Universe and the Ques.

The Ques are being uplifted by the Ques and Omega Psi Phi Fraternity Incorporated is uplifting.

Ω

The Ques live larger than life.

Ω

The Ques uplift, then we get it in.

Ω

The Founding Fathers are channels/vessels for the physical manifestation of the divine principles of Manhood, Scholarship, Perseverance, and Uplift.

Ω

Omega guides us. Omega's presence is wherever we go, in whatever we are doing. Omega is always ready to give comfort to us, help us, and uplift us with the right hand of righteousness.

Ω

The Ques do not player hate -- we elevate.

Ω

Friendship is essential to soul and manhood is essential to upholding strong values.

Do not ever forget Que, Omega Psi Phi Fraternity Incorporated is always and in all ways greater than you think it is.

Ω

Omega Psi Phi Fraternity Incorporated is the ultimate brotherhood.

Ω

We are the Ques; we are the epitome of confidence and enthusiasm.

Ω

Omega Psi Phi is the best college fraternity in the United States and the World.

Ω

Hopping is a jumping activity that stimulates all cells of the body simultaneously. Hopping and marching helps the Ques stay in fighting trim.

Ω

God sent the Ques to Uplift Omega Psi Phi Fraternity Incorporated, Black America, America, Africa, and the World and Ques we have been doing a great job. It is not about necessarily about the Ques, it is about the Creator expanding through the Ques and everyone else; however, with the Ques, the Creator is expanding at its most accelerated rate.

The Ques are infinitely powerful, loving, and extremely intelligent.

Ω

Omega Psi Phi Fraternity Incorporated is a strong and virile organization.

Ω

Hope is alive and well in Omega Psi Phi Fraternity Incorporated.

Ω

The Ques have successfully mentored youth and young black men to become contributing members of society -- a lot of the young men have grown up to be Ques.

Ω

The Ques are leaders that lead themselves and others into purposeful, powerful, and productive action.

Ω

BE OWT as much as you can, by all the means you can, in all the ways you can, at all the places you can, during all the times you can, for as many Ques as you can, for as long as you can. Then you will be able to obtain the glory that Omega Psi Phi Fraternity Incorporated, the Founding Fathers, and the Creator mean for you to have.

The Ques love paying dues in October, renewing our commitments to Omega Psi Phi Fraternity Incorporated.

Ω

Omega Psi Phi is proof of life. Our Founding fathers gave birth to Omega Psi Phi and now they live forever in our hearts and minds. Omega Psi Phi is a light that comes down from Heaven, for which a Que may live forever. Through his actions, a Que will give life though Omega Psi Phi, which will, in turn, give light to the World, for life.

Ω

Omega Psi Phi Fraternity Incorporated is about -- brotherhood (brotherly love).

Ω

The Ques who understand Omega Psi Phi walk close with God; the Ques are people that know and love God.

Ω

The quickest way to change Omega Psi Phi Fraternity Incorporated is to be of service to the Ques and others. Show that your brotherly love can make a difference in the lives of the Ques and others; thereby the Ques and someone else's love can make a difference in your life. By each of us doing this and working together we positively change Omega Psi Phi Fraternity Incorporated, and the World, one inner person at a time.

20

The Ques are masters of enthusiasm who possess unlimited enthusiasm.

Ω

Omega Psi Phi Fraternity Incorporated retains its splendor.

Ω

There is no accident that you are a Que. The Ques are alive at this time, gloriously displaying the power and presence of OMEGA. OMEGA has happened in our life for a positive purpose.

Ω

Once a Que, always a Que; the Ques wouldn't have it any other way.

Ω

The Ques and our families live in infinite abundance and infinite prosperity.

Ω

All men come to Omega Psi Phi to test their manhood to see if it is real. Only by becoming subject to the physical influences of the Omega Process and the laws of the Omega Process can a man know for certain if he really possess that manhood. Through the Omega Process, the man is tested and the result is self-realization and power. This is the purpose of the Omega Process.

Que God:

A Christian Manhood -- the aim of the frat is the high spiritual attainment expressed with high energy intensity -- the same ideal Jesus the Christ expressed.

Ω

Omega Psi Phi Fraternity Incorporated helps the Ques rise to the higher level of love and enthusiasm.

Ω

The Ques are infinitely powerful spiritual beings meant to create great things in Omega Psi Phi Fraternity Incorporated and on the Earth. Our greatness is not usually accomplished in bold actions, but in singular acts of kindness between the Ques and others. It is the little things that count, because they are more spontaneous and show in a better way who and what we truly are.

Ω

The Ques sons want to grow up to be Ques. Our sons are the future foundation of Omega Psi Phi Fraternity Incorporated. This is how the Ques will live on.

Ω

Omega Psi Phi Fraternity Incorporated is the vehicle to a purposeful life and a significant positive growth experience for the Ques.

22

The stages of OMEGA evolution:

Lamp - Que Dog - Omega Man - Que God

Ω

The Ques are Atomic Gods!

Ω

As the Ques expand; Omega Psi Phi Fraternity Incorporated expands.

Ω

A Que fears no man or experience.

Ω

The Ques have been and are doing "God's will."

Ω

The Ques are some of the best friends on Earth.

Ω

The Ques teach one another the valuable principle of humility.

Ω

Sometimes prayer to God is answered through the Ques.

The Ques and our families are automatically blessed, because we are distribution points for blessings to flow to others.

Ω

The Ques and are there if you need to talk or need some help. You are a Que; you have help for the rest of your life.

Ω

Although our goal was to leave ordinary being and come to Omega Psi Phi to become a Que; our greatest goal is to leave Omega Psi Phi as a Que and bring uplift to the world.

Ω

The Ques performing service builds positive karma in the name of Omega Psi Phi.

Ω

Omega Psi Phi Fraternity Incorporated is synonymous with greatness.

Ω

The Ques welcome the Ques and take care of one another; this is why the Ques feel safe with one another.

Ω

The Ques are gifted and talented.

Omega Psi Phi Fraternity Incorporated has created a majority of positive karma.

Ω

When you are working for Omega Psi Phi there may be situations that may appear to be problems, challenges, or obstacles. In actuality, there are no problems, challenges, or obstacles there are only opportunities. All thoughts and communication about Omega Psi Phi and the Ques must be framed in a positive and active manner to reach the opportunity that creates positive change.

Ω

The Ques are entrepreneurs and businessman; experts in capital creation that know how to make something out of nothing.

Ω

The Ques minds and spirits are stronger than our environment.

Ω

The highest purpose of our OMEGA connections is -- love.

Ω

The Ques are leaders in civil rights and have worked with Dr. Martin Luther King Jr. to secure civil rights for our community and all Americans.

The Ques are hardcore. A reason being is to provide our loved ones with safety and security.

Ω

The Ques have the best teamwork possible.

Ω

Omega Psi Phi Fraternity Incorporated has helped the Ques be better men.

Ω

The Ques support the brothers faithfully when the brothers have family members that transition.

Ω

The Ques are politicians; a Que has run for president twice and mentored our first African-American president. Many Ques have held local, state, and national office.

Ω

What is important is how we show our love for our Founders by the way we treat each other like brothers and friends.

Ω

The Ques are great husbands and win the "Husband of the Year" Award.

The Ques respect one another.

Ω

The Ques love one another <u>non-judgmentally and unconditionally.</u>

Ω

The Ques, our families, and guests are blessed and highly favored.

Ω

Omega Psi Phi Fraternity is real.

Ω

The Ques share our resources -- unselfishly.

Ω

The Ques use technology to uplift the family, community, America, and the World, to do God's job for us and to facilitate brotherly love.

Ω

Always remember, the Ques are always, and in all ways, greater than we think we are.

Ω

The Ques are spiritual warriors.

The Ques do not judge one another or others; this is one of the things our friends love about us.

Ω

The Ques know what it takes to be a friend.

Ω

The Ques are admired, loved, and respected in and outside of America.

Ω

The Ques have a significant role in God's Divine plan to positively change America and when America changes, the World will change.

Ω

When you work for Omega Psi Phi Fraternity you grow spiritually, and as a Que.

Ω

The Ques are part of the creative elite; the talented tenth of the population. The Omega Process created some of the best and the brightest of the human race.

Ω

The Ques are a super-human part of God.

The Ques are as mentally strong and spiritually strong as men can be and physically the Ques are in fighting trim.

Ω

The Ques are heroes to the adults and the children.

Ω

The Ques can persevere through any experience, on an individual or fraternal level.

Ω

The Ques have fun doing community service with the Ques, their families, and guests.

Ω

When the Ques participate in service, we make a huge difference in America and the World, one person at a time.

Ω

The Ques operate between excellence and perfection.

Ω

The Founding Fathers are men of high professional accomplishment that always worked tirelessly for OMEGA. Look at Founding Fathers as a true example of scholarship, career, family, and serving OMEGA.

The Ques are Omega Men on a mission.

Ω

The Ques do it the biggest IT can be done.

Ω

The Ques are elder brothers to the human family.

Ω

Grow, laugh, live, love, and play with the Ques forever.

Ω

The Ques are as brave and as courageous as men can be.

Ω

Being of a Que empowers you to overcome any weakness.

Ω

The Ques are fantastic lawyers that helped advance the civil rights struggle and have helped me, my family, and Ques I know out of legal difficulties and impossibilities.

Ω

The Ques throw some of the best parties on the planet.

The Ques are Transformers:

As we transform Omega Psi Phi, we transform Black America, America, and the World around us, and so, by stages, the whole future of humanity.

All it takes to expand Omega Psi Phi is one Que. One Que trying, and then because of that, another Que evolves for the better. The way we continue positive expansion of Omega Psi Phi is to begin with one Que, one will become two, which will become three, which become four, and so on. This is the way we continue to affect major expansion in Omega Psi Phi Fraternity Incorporated.

Ω

Blessed are the Ques in Omega Chapter.

Ω

God has vested the Ques with Godlike qualities -- maximized.

Ω

Omega Psi Phi Fraternity Incorporated is an expression of maximum enthusiasm, maximum energy.

Ω

The Ques are infinitely powerful spiritual beings manifested through the Royal Purple and Old Gold.

31

As steel sharpens steel, so does one Omega Man sharpen and uplift another.

Ω

The Ques are men of nobility that live nobly as all real men do.

Ω

The Ques save, heal, redeem, and uplift Omega Psi Phi Fraternity.

** We always have and we always will. **

Ω

God is flowing directly to, expanding, and working through the Ques.

Ω

You are a Que, you are somebody!

Ω

The Omega Brand maintains its mystique and mystery.

Ω

The Ques are stewards charged with the obligation to leave Omega Psi Phi Fraternity Incorporated, our community and our World in a better way than we found it.

The Ques are happy to be fathers; the Ques are great dads!

Ω

The Ques are working to make America and the World a better/happier place in which to live.

Ω

A most important reason the Ques are in Omega Psi Phi Fraternity Incorporated is to either learn or teach, most times both; the Ques learn from and teach one another.

Ω

The Ques do what we need to do for ourselves and Omega Psi Phi Fraternity Incorporated, when we need to do it.

Ω

Friendship is essential to life!

Ω

Brotherhood and friendship are essential to the soul of the Ques.

Ω

Omega Psi Phi is a great processor of energy. Enthusiasm evolves out of Omega Psi Phi into each one of us. At the heart of Omega Psi Phi is this great magnetic energy that keeps pulling Ques to her again and again and again.

Omega Psi Phi Fraternity Incorporated is perfect; the Ques are striving for perfection.

Ω

Omega Psi Phi: the worldwide leaders of enthusiasm, uplift, and owtness!

Ω

Omega Psi Phi Fraternity Incorporated is in God and we, the Ques, are in Omega Psi Phi.

Ω

The Ques have incredible discipline....shaped by an incredible process.

Ω

The Omega Process is the ideal place for spiritual growth because of the benefit of our physical body. Opportunities to experience a full range of enthusiasm are ideally available. Our physical body allows us to train at our maximum potential.

Ω

Omega Psi Phi Fraternity Incorporated offers you Advanced Enthusiasm Training through the Omega Process and one of the highest levels of spiritual growth and fulfillment available in the world today.

The Ques inspire and motivate and inspire one another to greatness.

Ω

The way of Omega Psi Phi is not easy, yet it is the tuneful, the rhythmic, the beautiful, the lovely way.

Ω

For as much as Omega Psi Phi Fraternity Incorporated can and must do, it is ultimately the faith and determination of the Ques upon which this fraternity relies.

Ω

Blessed are the Ques for it will be written in the Book of Life they are Sons of God.

Ω

The Ques are uplifting America from her place of apostasy towards recognition of her Master, and when America changes, the World will change.

Ω

Being a Que is an infinite life adventure.

Ω

The Ques are super-heroes to our community.

35

The Ques know Ques they can trust with their house, money, car, and life.

Ω

The Ques are experts in making money and fundraising.

Ω

Act, watch, and bear witness to the Ques uplifting Omega Psi Phi Fraternity Incorporated, America, and the World.

Ω

Ques are the epitome of friendship and brotherly love.

Ω

The Ques produce a smile on their children's faces when they walk in the home.

Ω

The Ques are athletes and stay in fighting trim.

Ω

The Ques can handle Omega Psi Phi Fraternity Incorporated.

Ω

The Ques love OMEGA and GOD loves the Ques.

One of the Founding Father's goals for Omega Psi Phi was to be an organization that would inspire young men to excel at leadership. This is who we are, exceptional leaders in all fields.

Ω

The Ques do all we need to do for ourselves and Omega Psi Phi on any given day or night.

Ω

The Ques chose Omega Psi Phi Fraternity Incorporated for a reason, not for a season.

Ω

Ques are instruments of God's light in America, and the World.

Ω

Find out why you are here, you are a Que for a reason, find your purpose.

Ω

The Ques have been called to uplift the people to be more than what they think they can be.

Ω

The Ques are infinitely powerful spiritual beings manifested through the Royal Purple and Old Gold.

If a man has manhood and desires to know if he actually possesses perseverance, the man can come to Omega Psi Phi to be tested and apply himself in a physical challenge. Omega Psi Phi is a great school for overcoming certain weaknesses in ways that only Omega Psi Phi can. We apply ourselves through Omega Psi Phi to see that these weaknesses are truly overcome and strength is created. We can grow in Manhood, Scholarship, Perseverance, and Uplift and truly change.

Ω

When the Ques and our guests come together for an Omega party -- it's magic.

Ω

Omega Psi Phi Fraternity Incorporated is a living organism.

Ω

God loves the Ques, our families, and friends.

Ω

Our guests don't know why, but they can't stay away. The Ques are compelled to come back for more, it never gets old. This is the secret, this is why: an OMEGA party is a form of Heaven in the now!

Ω

Every Que is valuable and all Ques are worthy.

The Ques are <u>Special Forces</u> for the Creator.

Ω

Que Dogs, Omega Men, and Que God's of the World unite.

Ω

Omega Psi Phi Fraternity Incorporated has helped powerful spiritual beings (men) elevate to infinitely powerful spiritual beings (Ques).

Ω

Omega Psi Phi Fraternity Incorporated has been destined to live forever.

Ω

As Ques, in our search for truth, all paths lead to friendship, the spirit of Omega Psi Phi Fraternity Incorporated.

Ω

100 Years Hard: Omega Psi Phi Fraternity Incorporated has been pre-ordained to exist eternally, as long as there are humans, there will be the Ques!

Ω

The Ques are meant to go out into the World, get resources, bring them back, and use to advance Omega's causes.

Omega Psi Phi Fraternity Incorporated is an ideal.

Ω

*The Ques are **bold enough** to cause a positive difference in the face of this Earth and the consciousness of her people.*

Ω

Omega Psi Phi Fraternity Incorporated is a gift from God to the Ques. The gift of Omega Psi Phi God gives us comes with a catch. We are to give the gift of service back.

Ω

Life is tough, that's why God gave the Ques perseverance.

Ω

Omega Psi Phi is about friendship and service -- not parties.

Ω

The Ques love one another without judgment or conditions.

Ω

Unselfish living is serving the Ques and others without any self-centered motives. The Ques live unselfishly, so we lead a life that's most worth living.

The Ques, our families, and friends live in abundance, prosperity, and fun.

Ω

We are all collectively bonded, by the silk bond, to each other while in Omega Psi Phi, bonded in this one ultimate purpose: to learn to love one another completely -- Friendship Is Essential To The Soul.

Ω

Omega Psi Phi is the ultimate experience for our souls. It is ultimate because our souls evolve faster through Omega Psi Phi than anywhere else. Our life condition is greatly accelerated because we are Ques.

Ω

By giving enthusiasm to the Ques, we receive and experience a tremendous enthusiasm from Omega Psi Phi Fraternity Incorporated.

Ω

The Founding Fathers designed us to become as the Founding Fathers are, and have accelerated the Manhood, Scholarship, Perseverance, and Uplift within us. The Founding Fathers want us to draw on the enthusiasm of Omega Psi Phi to uplift America, and by knowing that we have the capability to do so, we can.

The Ques are Omega Men of distinction.

Ω

We are all Omega Men! All Omega Men's gain or loss affects all other Omega Men to some degree because we are all connected.

Ω

Be thankful each day for the great gift of the life of a Que. Savor fully the loveliness of the OMEGA experience. Ques always go through life truly appreciating it. A purpose of this fraternal life is joy and with spiritual understanding the Omega Psi Fraternity Incorporated experience is enhanced.

Ω

The Ques stay ready, so we don't have to get ready.

Ω

Everything is evolving for Omega Psi Phi exactly as it should be. And the ultimate destiny for the Ques is to uplift the World and then return to the Source, the Light, Pure Love.

Ω

Omega Oil spill....the barrel runneth over.

Ω

The Ques are not just a bunch of guys, we are an Omega Unit.

The Ques greatest weapon is our minds.

Ω

OMEGA knows no boundaries and never runs out. The closer we get to OMEGA, the closer we come to all the light, life, and love, and knowledge in the universe.

Ω

We should be glad we have the opportunity to be the Ques and serve Omega Psi Phi at this time. We should be happy of it and give thanks daily for it.

Ω

We come to Omega Psi Phi for the evolution of our soul into the conscious awareness of true friendship.

Ω

Que Oil is an elixir of life, right up there with water and juice.

Ω

The Ques are fulfilling the vision the Founding Fathers have for Omega Psi Phi Fraternity Incorporated.

Ω

Omega Psi Phi Fraternity Incorporated is an accelerator for the Creative Forces manifesting on the physical plane.

Omega Psi Phi Fraternity Incorporated is divinely inspired from the Creator through the Founders (the most honorable Dr. Ernest Everett Just, the most honorable Bishop Edgar Amos Love, the most honorable Professor Frank Coleman, and the most honorable Dr. Oscar James Cooper) for us, our families, our community, America, and the World to be uplifted. Ques, we have been doing an excellent to perfect job, be proud.

Ω

A Que Warrior has two professions; our career and holding up the Light of Omega so that she shines daily.

Ω

Omega Psi Phi is a Light that shines from beyond time itself!

Ω

The Ques are positive brothers that motivate you to do your best.

Ω

Many men were high achievers before they became Ques. However, the Omega Process is designed to develop us into a high achiever automatically, by becoming a Que!

Ω

We are here to help the Ques and others rise to the higher level of love and enthusiasm.

The Ques suppress our individual selfish natures so that our higher unselfish nature is in control. Living unselfishly brings about a resurrection and ascension of the higher self, which creates Heaven on Earth.

Ω

Like a thirsty animal in the desert who finally finds a water-hole and quenches its thirst. Omega Psi Phi finally quenches the thirst of the Ques when we march across the burning sands!

Ω

The Founders have been entrusted by God to ensure that our souls evolve positively through Omega Psi Phi! Our Founding Fathers are of the highest ideals as compared to many other souls. God holds the Founders in the highest of favor because they are the great examples of what humans need to do -- uplift!

Ω

The Omega Process is a spiritual, mental, emotional, and physical training program designed to accelerate the Manhood, Scholarship, Perseverance, and Uplift within us -- making us stronger.

Ω

As a Que you are not an ordinary life; you are leading an extra-ordinary life.

Every one of us is a blessing to the Omega Psi Phi. We are legendary throughout America for our abilities and uplift. We came up with one of the best answers to the meaning of life. Lift as we climb!

Ω

OMEGA is unique because she was designed by our Founding Fathers and God for the Ques to forever learn, serve, play, and grow with her. OMEGA was designed for us as the Ques to access enthusiasm to help us advance.

Ω

The Ques have perseverance inside so far beyond our wildest dreams. Anything we want to do we can do. Whatever we want to be we can be. It may take a little while, but if we want it, we can get it.

Ω

Sometimes a Que may need to be forgiven; sometimes a Que may need to forgive. However, it is better to avoid mistakes, than to seek forgiveness for words quickly spoken or actions quickly taken.

Ω

The four cardinal principals were first created in the Founders minds and spirits and then recreated in the physical. We are the living embodiment of Manhood, Scholarship, Perseverance, and Uplift.

Every Que is meant to be a leader. We should be encouraged to cultivate even more leadership within ourselves; I am continuing to do the same. We need to continue to lead Omega Psi Phi, America, and the World into a better age. We are to leave Omega Psi Phi, America, and the World a lot better than we found it. And remember, true leadership is not just about how well one leads the Ques -- leadership is also how well one builds other Ques to lead in a positive manner!

Ω

The Ques feel honored to attend chapter meetings and conduct the business of Omega Psi Phi Fraternity Incorporated.

Ω

When a Que lays hands on you or hugs you, it feels like a million volts of electricity going through your body, electric!

Ω

The Ques feel honored to attend chapter meetings and conduct the business of Omega Psi Phi Fraternity Incorporated.

Ω

God is the love, light, life, and the energy in Omega Psi Phi Fraternity. God is the source of Omega Psi Phi Fraternity and all enthusiasm.

The simple secret to achieving our continued success as Omega Psi Phi is perseverance. Naysayers, the negative ones that say it cannot be done, have always been around. However, throughout our Omega Psi Phi history, progress has been made by the Ques that have said, yes we can. And it does not take great Ques to achieve great things; just those of us Ques that are greatly dedicated to doing them.

Ω

The Ques did not create the turmoil within America's Black community. However, we were created with the purpose in mind of cleaning it up -- of uplifting. The freedom of one Black person is enough to change the whole World.

Ω

Omega Psi Phi was great before we even came to her; all we have to do is have the most fun and love possible keeping her growing.

Ω

We are free to choose and build our destiny in Omega Psi Phi. Our works and friendships in Omega Psi Phi shape the kind of feedback we get from Omega Psi Phi.

Ω

We come here to live Omega Psi Phi fully, to live it enthusiastically, and to find joy in our friendships .... to use our Omega Psi Phi experience to expand and magnify our lives.

48

The Omega War Chapters:

The Ques are soldiers that have served and protected America and the World. Omega Men are at the forefront contributing to the service of our country. Brother George E. Brice helped spearhead our involvement by road tripping from Howard to a number of other HBCU's to create enthusiasm for the establishment of African American officers' training program. Brice, Jesse Heslip, Campbell Johnson, and William I. Nelson persevered, eventually obtaining a meeting with President Woodrow Wilson because the War Department was not moving fast enough to train African American officers.

President Wilson was persuaded by the brothers to immediately establish the War Chapters. President Wilson authorized qualifying examinations at Howard and established a war chapter at Ft. Des Moines. A great number of African American officers were trained at Ft. Des Moines and a number of Omega men were among them. By the end of the program twenty-one Omega men had obtained officer commissions.

The training program was the predecessor of today's HBCU ROTC programs. Two of our Founders promptly entered the Officers' Training Camp at FT. Des Moines and were commissioned as First Lieutenants, both serving in WWI. Frank Coleman served honorably overseas. Edgar Love became a Chaplain; while in the army he had supervision over 3,000 men. We are a paramilitary force this is why we wear the camouflage and some of the real men in this world wear Gold Boots.

Ω

49

Omega East Star Edition: Parts 1-4

*It is God's burning desire for everyone to attain Christhood;
the spiritual condition of Divine-Human unity. It is
the Founding Fathers desire for the Ques to evolve our Christian
Manhood; the spiritual condition of Divine-Que unity.
The Ques are men of high spiritual attainment.*

*The aim of the fraternity is Christian Manhood; this is the divine
design within the Ques, for the Ques to reach the highest spiritual
attainment possible. Christian Manhood is synonymous with
Christ, Christhood, Christed, Christ Consciousness, Mind of
Christ, Christ Force, Perfection, Christ Consciousness, God
Consciousness, Nirvana, Ascension, At-one-ment, Enlightenment,
Divine-Human Unity, and Buddha hood. The Founding
Fathers were channels/vessels for the Ques expressing the
same ideal Jesus the Christ expressed, a Christian Manhood.*

*Jesus the Christ was a man that attained a Christian Manhood,
Christhood. Jesus' suffering aided in the resurrection and
ascension of his transformed self. Suffering dissolves the human
ego of men (self-centeredness, self-gratification, self-
righteousness, self-glorification, self-indulgence, self-
promotion, self-condemnation, self-interest, self-consciousness,
self-aggrandizement, self-exaltation, and self-conceit), so that
our higher spiritual nature can gain control. The Founding
Fathers mission was to create a brotherhood for humanity where
self-sacrifice and self-denial can overcome these selfish desires and
lead to the complete evolution of the Divine Nature within us.
Our "Initiation" denotes a self-sacrifice and self-denial which
overcomes these selfish desires and leads to a restoration with
the powerful Divine Nature within us as Ques.*

The Ques are many Jesus the Christ's. This is our Divine Design: A Christian Manhood.

Ω

For my Neo's and young brothers:

1. *Travel and see brothers within and outside of your yard, state or district.*

a. *Get to know brothers for who they are and their interests.*

b. *Get brothers number and call them; visit brothers outside of our events, these are friendship. Build your mailing and email lists.*

c. *Get knowledge, hops, chants, and marches.*

2. *Always come around the Ques with enthusiasm. Anything you do in Omega Psi Phi or life needs enthusiasm and excitement to be great.*

3. *Fill your Lamp: learn as much as you can, read:*

a. *History Book(s)*

b. *Ritual*

c. *The Black Apollo of Science: biography of **The Most Honorable Ernest Everett Just**.*

d. *The Shield, read and apply, it is for your uplift.*

e. *Know the Pearls, when talking about the Pearls, talk about the pearls in a sentence.*

f. *Learn about the chapter: History, members, successes and mistakes.*

g. *The Bible for inspiration; the Bible is: The record of a Holy One. The Bible is the symbolic account of the fall and restoration of the Human Soul to its Divine origins. Genesis is the symbolic testimony of humanity's fall from Heaven and paradise lost. Revelation is the symbolic testimony of humanity's restoration to Heaven and paradise found. Read it spiritually in order to understand it. The Bible should be read spiritually as if through God's eyes. When we read it prayerfully, it talks to us it reveals itself to us. By reading the Bible spiritually and prayerfully, versus literally, the Holy Spirit can guide us, the reader, the seeker, into spiritual truth. All knowledge and wisdom comes directly from God!*

* The more you learn: the more you will uplift yourself and the Ques; the more confident you will become and the more your purpose will reveal itself.

4. *Be the kind of brother you want to spend time around.*

5. *Work for Omega, when we work we grow spiritually and as a Que.*

6. *Discretion--no one knows the Ques business but the Ques.*

7. *The Ques work hard and smart, then play hard and smart. It's ninety percent work and ten percent owtness!*

8. *The Ques don't start trouble, we finish it.*

9. *Be there if the brothers need to talk or need some help. Seek to uplift one another, the student body, and the community, Be the man that other men aspire to be: high scholastics, fighting trim, and positive role models..*

10. *Treat women and our guests with respect.*

11. *High knees and low black!*

ΩΩΩΩ

52

Epsilon Beta -- the UPLIFT chapter: Parts: 1- 4

Omega is the end; the end is a new beginning.

William Lucky

Mark 3:17- to them, he gave the name Boanerges, which means Sons of Thunder.

Jay Poindexter

The Ques never hit one another in the face.

David Lee

Spend time with the Ques outside of our events.

Nook the Que

Ω

The first time you are owt with the Ques and love it. You will want to be owt with the Ques forever!

Abdel K. Muhammad,

Ω

I tell of Omegas greatness everywhere I go.

Andre Kilpatrick

ΩΩ

The brotherhood demonstrated by the Ques is duplicated by none.

Ω

The Spirit of Omega is in sync with all the Divine principles of the universe!

Ω

The veracity and the tenacity within the brotherhood is the seed that compels us to have high aspirations.

Ω

Love all, trust a few including the Ques, and do no harm to none as the principles of OMEGA are good and balanced.

Ω

All men of Omega Psi Phi Fraternity Incorporated are connected by oath, obligation and a rigorous pledge program. True men of Omega recognize that a transgression towards a friend is not friendship.

Andre marshall

Ω

Long live Omega Psi Phi and the sons she birthed....

Anthony Kelly

Ω

The Ques are getting bigger, stronger, and faster.

Anton White

ΩΩ

The Ques are of a different breed. We bleed the enthusiasm of the Royal Purple and Old Gold.

Ω

Long Live the Ques! Let us continue to live out the 4 cardinal principles, cherish the 4 pillars of faith, honor the 4 unwrittens, and love the 4 Founding Fathers.

Antwan Taylor

Ω

The Ques are great people.

Ayana Trice-Henderson

Ω

It does not matter whether we pledge graduate or undergraduate. Don't make that distinction; it is of little significance. Graduate or undergraduate does not make us a better Que. It is how we dedicate ourselves to Omega.

Baron Weston

Ω

No stimulus package required here! Understand that being a Que is a true form of wealth. A true brother will always be rich in the friendship that OMEGA offers. May we continue to be true brothers to one another.

Bomani Sundai

Ω

Brothers in true brotherhood are Omega Psi Phi fraternity's number one asset.

Carl Blunt

Ω

To the Omega Men who have taken the mantle of fatherhood, and done all the right things: without any reminders and sometimes no reward. The children are our future and you posses the keys to the future. Your good works have not gone unnoticed. I am not a father as of yet but when I do and I have any questions I will be knocking at your door.

Calvin Attoh

Ω

I don't care how he got here, once he is here, he is a Que.

Climent Edmond

Ω

We feel that we Omega Men are way out front in the area of civil rights, going back to the days when Roy Wilkins, Oliver W. Hill, James Nabrit, and Wiley Branton were first initiated as brothers. When you look at Benjamin Hooks, Rev. Jesse Jackson Sr., Vernon Jordan, and Gov. Douglas Wilder and other brothers, we feel that we are definitely ahead of the game.

C. Tyrone Gilmore

Ω

When I took on the task of being an OMEGA, it was not just for the college days or homecoming, it was for life! I live OMEGA every day, and when I enter the Omega Chapter, I will still continue to uplift OMEGA.

Dave Allsbrook

Ω

The Ques are wise and we use our wits.

David Barnes

ΩΩ

Omega is a monster: the most difficult fraternity in which to obtain membership!

Ω

I would die for you Que, and I AM not even asking you to die for me, just know I would die for you.

David Lee

Ω

I AM OMEGA and You Will Know Me:

I AM a member of Omega Psi Phi Fraternity and you will know that I AM not because I "threw up the hooks" but by the way I threw out intelligent solutions to the problems facing black people, America, and our World.

I AM an Omega Man and you will know that I AM not by the way I set out a "hop," "stomped" or "stepped" in the street but by the way I did not hesitate to step up to the plate when called to lay down my life for my brothers, my family or my community.

I AM an OMEGA and you will know that I AM not because you heard me bark out a call on the "yard" or in the club, but by the way I barked out truth to power even under threat of being clubbed.

I AM a Que and you will know that I AM not because you saw me wearing Royal Purple and Old Gold but because I am cloaked in the royal purple robe of self-sacrifice and self denial fighting for the goal of freedom for a people.

I AM OMEGA and you will know that I AM

not because you see a Greek letter branded on my bare arm or chest but because I am armed with a special brand of enthusiasm and self-discipline that gets things done.

I AM a member of the Omega Psi Phi Fraternity Incorporated and you will know that I AM not only because of what you see ON me but what you see IN me you will know that I AM. Not by the "hooks," the "hops" or the hieroglyphs but by the deeds done, the truth spoken, and the sacrifices made.

Yes, I am the man who believes that Friendship is Essential to the Soul.
I AM a man of OMEGA and you will know that I AM.

D. Michael Lyles, Jr.

ΩΩ

There is a place for mediocrity in our society, but not in OMEGA.

Ω

Omega Men in every community, stand out in every community.

Ω

Prove yourself to be a true Omega Man.

Ω

For he who would have a friend, must be one.

Ω

The Four Cardinal Principles do have consideration in their order of arrangement. In considering members in OMEGA, the first consideration is for manhood. This of course, in itself is character. First and foremost, a Que must be a man of sterling worth, with unsullied character. Secondly, is scholarship, which follows closely to the first? There is, of course, a place for all men in the economy of our colleges and country, but we want men whose intellectual ability is above average. Thirdly, of course, is perseverance which is that attribute of character which holds one steadfast to a purpose or to a cause. With these three characteristics, the individual is then ready to lend himself to the coexistence of his fellowman. Here we have the principle of uplift.

Edgar Love

Ω

If you are a man that was raised without values, OMEGA then becomes your values. If you were raised with values, Omega expands on them.

Eric White

Ω

Any institution which fails to render its need of service to society must lead a torturous and uncertain existence if indeed it continues to exist at all.

Ω

The only excuse for existence, the only raison d'etre of any public institution is the service it can render society. Any institution which fails to render its mead of service to society must lead a tortuous and uncertain existence if indeed it continues to exist at all.

Frank Coleman

Ω

Enthusiasm is a spiritual being. You cannot fake it, mask it, or hide it. If you have it, it is in you. Enthusiasm is in the Ques, massively!

Fredrick Banks

ΩΩ

Dog is God spelled backwards, when the Ques say dog we also mean God!

Ω

The Ques don't start trouble, we finish it.

Ω

The Ques work hard and smart, then play hard and smart.

Frederick Johnson & Endo

ΩΩ

Festive is the Ques personified.

Ω

The Ques follow God's will, don't quit, and always see it through.

Ω

Omega Psi Phi Fraternity Incorporated is the epicenter of friendship, the only reason we were created is to help others.

Fredrick Williams

Ω

Omega Prayer:

Oh God,
as we draw nigh and ask your blessings today, we reflect on the fell clutch of circumstance that brought us together as friends, molded us into neophytes, and permitted us to seek the great body of wisdom on the circle of life.

Oh God, we ask that you enlighten us to: exemplify MANHOOD, not based on age, the accumulation of material wealth or disrespect to womanhood, but rather by limiting one's travels on the wide road of foolishness, so that we as men, live nobly by finding the narrow road of righteousness and responsibility; to value SCHOLARSHIP, not merely as a means of financial prosperity, but rather so we, as scholars, serve as lamps on dark paths of ignorance; to embrace PERSEVERENCE, not with unbridled ambition, but through the undaunted pursuit of dream stars so that we, as industrious men, serve as golden examples of the necessity to hold fast to dreams; and to commit ourselves to UPLIFT, not to establish a debt of gratitude among the less fortunate, but rather so we, as "social engineers", construct a better world.

Finally, we ask oh God, that you allow us to recognize that OMEGA is an eternal quest; and therefore, all OMEGA MEN are linked by a mutual sense of relativity of purpose and action, requiring us to structure our behavior so that no criticism is levied on OMEGA.

As the African proverb states: I AM because we are; and because we are, therefore I AM. We ask these blessings in honor of our collective ancestors. In particular, we ask in the name of JUST, COOPER, COLEMAN, and LOVE, Founding Fathers of our beloved organization, Omega Psi Phi Fraternity Incorporated -- Amen.

Gary Flowers

ΩΩ

Ques do not live up to manhood -- we define it.

Ω

A Que is not the pinnacle of perfection, but God had to start somewhere.

Ω

The Ques live clean and unselfishly amongst the masses, shining brightly amongst those who know them.

Ω

A Que is a man marked with accountability and accomplishment, his swagger is charismatic and his confidence sinks down to the bone marrow. A Que is someone with tenacity that surpasses limits. One whose mind does not understand the meaning of words like impossible, quit, and surrender. And a Que is someone together you can live with and if need be die with, grow and raise your kids together with. Thorough immersion is in the True Omega Spirit. And it still perplexes men today; they wonder why we come into the fold in lines.

Ω

A Que is many men in one. As a brother, he lays his life for those he loves; he intimidates pretenders and always has a crust and a corner to sleep in. As an Omega he constantly imprints himself into history with such depth it rivals the brand in his chest. So many men think they know what a Que is. They do not know, but can feel the tenacity signified in a bark, the toil written deep within a march, and the blood, sweat, and tears when a song dog sets out a verse. This why most black males want to be a Que first!

Ω

A Que is the archetype of manhood in its true form. Not limited by fear, knowing it is the mind killer. A warrior, taking on the challenges of life, as if bred to do nothing else. Loyalty, second to none. The most copied, but never duplicated. A Que is one who must watch the walk and make sure it is upright, resolute, and true because even at his weakest and worse moment, everyone wants to be a Que.

Ω

A Que looks at adversity as natural way of life. He sees it as a way to define his quality when others show vulnerability. He is a shining light of hope when others falter. He is a lamp called to guide the masses to be more than what they thought they can be. Being owt is a mere by-product of his existence.

Gilbert Richardson

Ω

Omega Men give respect to their elders, family, community leaders, fraternal brothers, and those that have influenced them regardless of how they feel about them individually.

Hank Beatty

Ω

It is obvious therefore that we cannot afford to become smug or complacent. We are faced with the ongoing challenge of uplifting Omega Psi Phi and our community and we must meet this challenge with our persistent dedication to the pursuit of excellence.

Harold Webb

Ω

VOICES OF OMEGA:

We have sent our most influential brothers across the country to enlighten America. Our bodies have been subjected to the cruelest violence. Our Lives have been affected with indignities never intended for mankind. Nevertheless, we have sent our most influential brothers across the country to enlighten America on the issues involved, decrying the oppressors and re-awakening America, the America which sprang from the Declaration of Independence, the America which in these latter fearful years has become the chief custodian of the democratic heritage among nations of the World. This we have done, for we know we cannot isolate ourselves, and that the most outstanding contribution we can make to the social order of the day is by seeing ourselves in relation to other men.

We know, too, that equal opportunity is inevitable and point with pride to those of our Brothers who have made personal sacrifices for us all. Z. Alexander Looby in Nashville was hanged in effigy; Charles Gomillion, under threat of life, sparks the leadership of the Tuskegee Improvement Association; John H. Calhoun of Atlanta was jailed for opposing the denial of basic rights; Wiley Branton fights doggedly against great odds in Arkansas for what must be; Edward T. Graham must serve as an inspiration to those in Miami, Florida. There is no need to go on, for the mere mention of those few names should make us realize what some of our brothers are doing, and that it is the job for the rest of us to give meaningful support to their efforts. While all of us cannot give our blood, we can make more financial sacrifices. Are we going to pass our brothers unnoticed as they labor in the "desert of ignorance?"

Herbert Tucker

Ω

Ques let us not forget who we are, by whom we were created, and whom we represent. The Ques have no choice but to be ALMIGHTY, because our Father is! It is our duty to encourage another brother who might be facing a giant in their life! We are loved and we have a purpose here!

Jacques Miles

Ω

I thank God for everything that I have been given. I AM a proud member of Omega Psi Phi Fraternity Incorporated. I understand that nothing should be taken for granted and that all of us have a responsibility to use our gifts and talents to change and impact the lives of others.

James Peters

Ω

A Brother's Dream:

A Brother dreamed of one day becoming a man.
A man dreamed of entering into Omega Land.
To bond with the chosen with lamp in hand,
Searching for that eternal light.
To be amazed by its illuminating sight.
To see it through its ups and downs.
To stare at danger without a frown.
For courageous is he that makes it to the land of purple and gold.
To reap Omegas mysteries, within thine soul.
To live noble as real men do.

To be thy brother's keeper is what I ask of you.
To make this pledge, one must know the true tradition of "See It Through"
Remember you are facing just what other men have met.
When you think about quitting tell your body, "not quite yet".
Pain is temporary and those who precede us knew this to be true.
And pave this road for me and you.
To make a man you have to be a man.
To pledge a man you should have been pledged.
To live the life of a lamp is to live on the edge.
To be a true brother, you should choose to pledge.
At last a brother dreamed of this mystical thing.
To the great fraternity of Omega Psi Phi do not change a Brothers Dream.

James Thomas

Ω

Ques have the ability to be owt on all sides; socially, in education, in work, and in philanthropy.

Jean Claude Aurel

Ω

My mind is on Omega Psi Phi - my heart is into Omega Psi Phi - my soul is Omega Psi Phi - my worth to Omega Psi Phi -- priceless!

Jeffrey Carter

Ω

Find your niche - (the activity in the Omega Psi Phi in which you can contribute your gifts and talents for the greatest good).

Jeff Mckamey

Ω

To be a Que is to KNOW that before the foundation of the world WE were chosen to do what the average man does not have the capacity to even think of. That is, leading in a unique manner that another can never imitate or duplicate. They can only contemplate with the remote hope of possibly being able to demonstrate.

Johnny Lynch

Ω

Omega Psi Phi Fraternity Incorporated is one blood and one body. We are one body with many functions.

Johnny Watters

Ω

As Ques, we must go through life working to improve ourselves and not prove ourselves.

Larry Childs

ΩΩ

Ques are born in destiny; many are called but ONLY a few are chosen.

Ω

Let us continue to stand firm on our four cardinal principles and "See It Through," plus anchor to become "Bridge Builders" so when we say our last goodbye, we can shout, we'll love Omega Psi Phi!

Lawrence Marshall

Ω

More than any single experience I have ever had, becoming an Omega Psi Phi prepared me for life. Prepared me for those moments I didn't think I'd finish my PhD. Prepared me for fatherhood, for how to raise, care for, and discipline children. And most importantly it prepared me for now--when it seems as if the bills don't stop coming, the challenges of raising a family of seven in a Depression never cease, when every day a new hurdle appears, a new obstacle looms large. Twenty years and one day later I wonder where I would be without the Ques. Long live the Sons of Blood and Thunder. Long live Omega Psi Phi Fraternity!

Lester Spence

Ω

Omega Is:

Omega is a beacon of hope
Omega is broadening ones scope
Omega is giving when there is a need
Omega is being exemplary in your word and your deed
Omega is every brother caring
Omega is every brother sharing
Omega is Cooper, Coleman, Love, and Just

Omega is taking a stand whenever you must
Omega is earnestly facing life day by day
Omega is being prudent in what you think and say
Omega is this feeling we have of kin
Omega is knowing when to compromise and when to bend
Omega is that mighty Royal Purple and Old Gold
Omega is that something that strengthens your soul
Omega is knowing your own true identity
Omega is an ideal that hopefully will extend throughout infinity

Lynn Beckwith, Jr.

Ω

Some of the best brothers God ever blew life into are the Ques.
God breathed life into the Ques November 17th 1911.

Maceo Rainey

Ω

The Omega Man:

The different sides of you
I constantly visualize
I see a man
That will not compromise
He is the man that provides
In the center of the family
He stands
Like the tallest strongest tree
He is respected by many
He is diligent and true
Faithful and precise

he's Omega, he's you
You enhance in your potential
You continue to stand
Through every disappointment
You remain, the Omega Man
In spite of oppositions
When faced with everything and more
You are Omega
Standing for all those before
Continue to enlighten
All that you meet
Whether it's the politician
Or a shoeless person on the street
You are the essence of strength
The essence of a power some may not understand
You are the essence of manhood
You are the Omega Man

Madonna Jackson

Ω

Omega Psi Phi: *One of the greatest stories that was ever told*

One of the greatest stories that was ever told
The founding of the Royal Purple and Old Gold
Four great young men who couldn't have had a way to know
That their fledgling fraternity would grow and grow
What they started at Howard has not yet ceased
A tenacious dog was unchained, a great power unleashed
Many great Men have followed them since they created this Wonder
Consisting of Omega Men, Que Dawgs, or, put simply, Sons of Blood and Thunder
Our mission is to cure America and the World's ills with our deeds
Fight poverty, homelessness, illiteracy -- whatever your needs
Our strength lies not in number, but in true brotherhood

Warm bodies are useless, they do our cause no good
Though the path to earn, this may be quite rough,
We can't make you men but real men do make Us
Don't seek to gain entrance by using the back door
You must understand, ANYTHING WORTH HAVING IS WORTH
WORKING FOR
Were Just, Love, Cooper, and Coleman at this moment alive
We hope they'd be pleased that their creation has survived
We pledged to make this stronger, never surrender, always persevere
There's not a wrong we wouldn't right for our Omega Dear

Marcus A. Johnson

Ω

Whether financial, domestic, social or political, the Ques meet
trouble squarely face to face. Ques refuse to let problems neither
define nor defile them; we tell problems what they can and cannot
do. Ques overcome problems to build strength. We are
resourceful and optimistic and always view the glass as half-full
rather than half empty. Ques seek solutions and Divine counsel
in our choices. Teach our daughters how good a man should treat
them by example and teach sons how to be men and accountable.
Married Ques provide love, affection and security to wives by
any Godly means necessary.

Mark Oliphant

Ω

We are invincible Que Dog's, Omega Men, and Que God's that can accept any challenge and meet it face-to-face without wincing or crying out loud.

Medgar Clark

Ω

Ques are always striving for perfection. The ultimate aim of the Blackman is to become a reflection of ALLAH. We learn the very principles of GODHOOD on the path of OMEGA. A Que is an upright husband, strong father figure, and serves God.

Michael Muhammad

Ω

Omega Psi Phi Fraternity Incorporated is greater than any of us.

Michael Winchester

Ω

The Ques are the light, sent by God to purify Greekdom of all its myths and stereotypes.

Mike Osifalujo

ΩΩ

Ques fear not -- pain, severe hardship nor death!

Ω

Omega Psi Phi Fraternity Incorporated is the vehicle to a purposeful life.

Michael Thorton Jr.

Ω

A Que bears the weight of OMEGA and the world on his shoulders, but the burden is made lighter when he has the help of his friends.

Perron Thrurston

Ω

To the men of Omega Psi Phi! Even if you do not have children, you are still recognized on Father's day as a mentor to our African-American youth. We must continue to be steadfast as we show the world that African-American men matter and care about our families and our communities. Let us continue to lift as we climb and uplift others.

Peter Boykin

Ω

We felt that with Manhood, the next important requisite is Scholarship, which is the key to the kind of men we should have to build a strong and virile organization, especially since it is a college organization.

Oscar Cooper

Ω

Thoroughly immersed in the True Omega Spirit:

Since our founding on Friday evening, November 17th, 1911, the men of OMEGA PSI PHI have remained true to our four cardinal principals. We always stand firm on our MANHOOD. We will always take care of our responsibilities as fathers, brothers, and mentors and will always be willing to serve in these roles at a moment's notice. SCHOLARSHIP is maintained at all times. Not only do OMEGA men excel academically by being OWTspoken and InQUEsitive during class, but we are street smart, which allows us to connect to our communities. In the darkest of times, we exhibit PERSERVERANCE. No matter the hardship, from financial worries to family difficulties, OMEGA men will always be around. We are the last man, when the rest fall, OMEGA men still stand. With these principles firmly rooted in our whole being, we UPLIFT. OMEGA men help our youth, brothers, and women by serving as coaches, teachers, advisors, etc....we are ready to serve in any capacity, not because it is mandated that we do so, but because it is our calling to improve the quality of our lives and others. So it is easy to see why "FRIENDSHIP IS ESSENTIAL TO THE SOUL." We attract people by exhibiting massive amounts of ENTHUSIASM, whether we are new to the fraternity or have dedicated many years. We live for OMEGA and we die for OMEGA, a passion that manifests itself to how we treat others. And when we are called to OMEGA chapter, to be closer to our creator, the roads in Heaven will be ROYAL PURPLE and OLD GOLD, RΩΩF!!!! BE OWT and stay THOROUGHLY IMMERSED!!!!

Quinton Arthur

Ω

I LOVE YOU BRO!:

One day a woman's husband died, and he was an OMEGA MAN. On that clear, cold morning, in the warmth of their bedroom, the wife was struck with the pain of learning that sometimes there isn't "anymore". No more hugs, no more special moments to celebrate together; Mardi Gras, Boat Rides, Step Shows, no more sex, no more phone calls, no more texting, no more "just one minute." Sometimes, what we care about the most gets all used up and goes away, never to return before we can say good-bye, say I love you brother."

So while we have it, its best we love it, care for it, fix it when it's broken and heal it when it's sick. This is true for Omega Men, old cars, and children with bad report cards, and dogs with bad hips, and aging parents and grandparents. We keep them because they are worth it, because we are worth it.

Some things we keep -- like a good bro who moved away or a brother who just lost his wife. There are just some things that make us happy, no matter what.

Life is important, like people we know who are special. And so, we keep them close! Suppose one morning you never wake up, do all your friends know you love them? Say it today so you won't forget.

I LOVE YOU BRO!

I was thinking...I could die today, tomorrow or next week, and I wondered if I had any wounds needing to be healed, friendships that needed rekindling or three words needing to be said.

I LOVE YOU BRO!

Let every one of your friends know you love them. Even if you think they don't love you back, you would be amazed at what those three little words and a smile can do. And just in case I'm gone tomorrow.

I LOVE YOU!

Live today because tomorrow is not promised. We will enter Omega Chapter one day. If you stay ready you don't have to get ready....LIFE IS GOOD live it NOW!!

I LOVE YOU BRO!

Ron Blanch

Ω

As Omega Men, we should "pledge" OMEGA every day. Be it respect, be it uplifting the less fortunate or those seeking to climb from their present state, promoting scholarship in our communities and our homes, or living our creed which shines the Light of Omega upon those we touch!

Roy Byrd

Ω

Omega Psi Phi was fashioned from ideas and discoveries which originated in the spirit world. Everything in Omega Psi Phi came from the spirit world. Omega Psi Phi possesses a soul!

Roy Shepard

Ω

2011 to 2111:

What is for certain is that we will NOT be here to see 2111 (our Bi-Centennial). So what we do today, will plant the seeds that will bear fruit a hundred years from now. Brothers Cooper, Coleman, Love, and Just imagined greatness for Omega Psi Phi but could they have measured the impact on society that this fraternity has had, on that stormy night in 1911? What we know is that they looked around and saw what they didn't like, and changed the World. Let's not let our vision of Omega Psi Phi be limited, we must continue to expand her. If we look at her with full 20/20 vision, we will see that Omega Psi Phi has touched the lives of not just African-America, but America in all aspects, and we can too, change the World. Our roots have owt-grown many organizations that have come before, and after us. These organizations, by the hundreds of thousands, have come and gone in the last one hundred years. Outside of the Black Church, and the NAACP, there are not many Black organizations or businesses that have stood that test of time. So let us continue to define not only ourselves, but our culture and our race. It is our duty to continually to "lift"....!

Over the last 100 years, we have gone from traveling on horseback to walking on the moon. Omega Psi Phi has been there for every transition, often leading the way. Because it was the horse that carried the Honorable Colonel Charles Young to Washington, DC, and today, Bro. Major General Charles Bolden heads NASA. This is who we are, exceptional leaders in all of our fields.

So many of us remember what Apostle Paul said to Timothy, as we were seeking Omega Psi Phi. So let us continue to light that fire, and let Omega's Flame shine brightly....as we make 2011 the most powerful year in the history of Omega Psi Phi to date.

If you cannot attend, sponsor a mentee to go, whether it is a nephew, kid on the block, or someone on the team that you coach. We have to let our young men see the fullness of Omega Psi Phi, especially when she is at her best. They need us more now than ever.

Sean Long

Ω

All men of OMEGA should understand we have a higher calling to serve without excuses. Let us continue to build our foundation on friendship and serve without judgment.

Sedrick Spencer

Ω

Long live Omega Psi Phi, a fraternity of friends.

Shelvis Lewis

Ω

I AM DA BRUHS:

I will conquer what has never been conquered. Defeat will not be in my creed. I will believe where all those before me have doubted. I will always endeavor to uphold the prestige, honor and respect of my team. I have trained my mind and now my body will follow!

WHO AM I? ....
I AM DA BRUHS

I will acknowledge the fact that I am an elite warrior who arrives at the cutting edge of battle by any means at my disposal. I accept the fact that my team expects me to move further, faster and fight harder than our opponents. Never shall I fail my comrades. I will always keep myself mentally alert, physically strong and morally straight and I will shoulder more than my share of the task whatever it may be. One hundred percent and more

WHO AM I? ....
I AM DA BRUHS

Gallantly, will I show the world that I am a specially selected and a well trained warrior. My heart and my soul will be the fuel to carry my body when my limbs are too weary. I will never falter, I will never lose focus as long as there is hope in my mind and my heart still beats. I will never give in to the evil that is weakness and I will fight that evil with my dying breath.

WHO AM I? ....
I AM DA BRUHS

Energetically, will I meet my enemies, no one will challenge me, none will stop me from my goal. I shall defeat them on the field of battle for I am better trained and will fight with all my might. Surrender is not a Champion's word. I will never leave a fallen comrade to fall at the hands of my enemy and under no circumstances will I ever surrender.

WHO AM I? ....
I AM DA BRUHS

Readily will I display the discipline and strength required to fight on to my objective and I will complete my mission. I will rise if I fall. I will rip the heart from my enemy and leave it beating on the ground if need be. My enemy need not fear me but he will respect me and if he does not.... I will give respect first, and then make him respect me with all that I have to give.

WHO AM I? ....
I AM DA BRUHS

History will remember my name and does not have to be kind. For I will have denied his criticisms and put in my own praise, No one will define me, no one will tell me what I can achieve, none will say I have not given all I have to give and none will take my glory.

WHO AM I? ....
I AM DA BRUHS

81

DEDICATED TO THE BRUHS

Sifiso Mkhize

ΩΩ

MANHOOD -- *the basic principle of responsibility.*

SCHOLARSHIP --*the acquisition of knowledge and the effective use of it.*

PERSEVERANCE -- *effort only releases its true rewards after one refuses to quit.*

UPLIFT --*the movement for improvement on behalf of the community.*

ΩΩ

We are all merely visitors briefly passing through this world. While in this world do good deeds for Omega Psi Phi Fraternity and others, which are pleasing to the Supreme Basileus of the Universe.

Ω

Omega Psi Phi Fraternity Incorporated is a blessing from the Supreme Basileus of the universe given 2 our beloved Founding Fathers for Omega Men to enjoy and love for all eternity.

Ω

Omega Psi Phi should only enhance the character that is already within you; character which exemplify Manhood, Scholarship, Perseverance, and Uplift.

Ω

The men of Omega Psi Phi's soul purpose on Earth is 2 preserve black intellectual manhood. All brothers must accept this duty as their ultimate goal in life.

Ω

LOVE' Omega Psi Phi 'JUST' as our Founding Fathers loved Omega Psi Phi. Exemplify the same friendship Dr. COOPER and Professor COLEMAN had while in high school together.

Ω

According to your deeds, your life in Omega Chapter will be blessed with rewards to enjoy throughout all eternity.

Sloan Toussaint Baptiste

Ω

May the grace of the Lord stay with us as stay dedicated to living by the Four Cardinal Principals established by our Founders.

Steven Millner,

Ω

Power of a Que:

Many don't understand the qualities
That an Omega Man must possess
If you don't you never will
It's the secret of frat success

Could it be that unique style
The way he can arouse an ear
Could it be his power
That other fraternities fear

Could it be his passion
From the way his story is told
Could it be a simple touch
That turns everything to gold

Or maybe it's the way
He treats me like a queen
Or maybe it's his out-spoken charm
That keeps him in my dreams

Maybe this is something
Others would not understand
A tradition that continues today
The power of the Omega Man.

Tanneka Howard

Ω

By God's grace and divine mercy everything always go the Ques way; so we can be in the best position possible to help others to have things go their way.

Terence Hamilton & Endo

Ω

Remember Que to always lift your lamp by the Golden Door-- every Que will give you some light to further illuminate your lamp's fire. We must encourage each other and share some light among ourselves. The Ques are Lamps for light, life, and love.

Terry Pickens

ΩΩ

When the Ques hop, we hop with enthusiasm and precision!

Ω

At Least two Ques should be hopping at our parties at all times.

Terry Robinson

Ω

The Ques want to get to know you.

Tim Tyler

Ω

True story....to all my Ques, proudly marked as a son of blood and thunder and stained with the Royal Purple and Old Gold. May

the love that binds us together burn eternally.
Live nobly, friends!

Tre Hodge

Ω

The Ques are true African warriors.

Troy Collins

Ω

Members versus Men:

*The Greek Letter Societies among our group appear to have
entered into a period of mad competition for obtaining members.
Pledges are increasing in numbers. Scarcely a student on the
college campus but wears a pledge pin or a frat pin. Are the
fraternities forgetting their original high standards? Can
it be said that every man who enters college is of Fraternity
material? If in any place, Omega has entered this mad race for
members, pause and consider.* **The value of our Fraternity is not
in numbers, but in men, in real brotherhood. Eight men
thoroughly immersed in the True Omega Spirit are far greater
assets than eighty with lukewarm enthusiasm.** *If any chapter has
reached the maximum in numbers for efficient work and brotherly
cooperation, let it initiate each year only the number of men
leaving the chapter by way of graduation or otherwise,* **Men, real
men of Omega caliber, strive for that which is most difficult of
attainment. Keep OMEGA the most difficult Greek letter**

society in which to obtain membership and rest assured that Omega Material will never be found lacking!

Walter Maczyk

Ω

Everyone can't be the Ques, there has to be something else for other's to do.

William Harris

ΩΩ

Beloved brothers, as we celebrate our 100th year of existence, let us continue to dedicate ourselves to the vision of our beloved Founders. The Founders knew that we would be coming their way. They saw all of us who now claim the Royal Purple and Old Gold. They knew we would be coming because their vision was the Creator wish. They made it to the mountain top and they looked over and they saw a sea of men dedicated to "Friendship is Essential to the Soul". Long live the glorious Omega Psi Phi Fraternity Incorporated!

Ω

Beloved Brothers, John Maxwell one of my favorite authors writes that, "we overestimate the event and underestimate the process." As we journey through our next 100 years, let us remember the intent that our beloved Founding Fathers had when they came together. It was to continue the development of this great institution, to further the tenets of this institution, and to celebrate what we hold dear, which is our friendship as brothers. Every decade we have accomplished great things as an organization: the establishment of the celebration of African American/Black history month, our beloved hymn "Omega Dear", our first national headquarters, our support of the NAACP, a constitutional convention, our national monument at Howard, the completion of our pledge to the UNCF. Throughout these decades thousands of Omega men have passed our way and have contributed to this great institution we call Omega Psi Phi. Many are still with us and many are now in Omega Chapter. It is for these Omega Soldiers that I write this uplift. They demand that as we journey our next 100 years, even to forever, that we stand firm, and that we persevere in continuing to maximize Omega Psi Phi's fullest potential. We must remember that one of the greatest battles any organization can wage is against that failure occurs from the inside, not the outside. Therefore it is with due diligence that we must prevail as a brotherhood; we owe it to them, we owe it to ourselves, and we owe it to the future brothers who will one day sit in our places as brothers of the most noble Omega Psi Phi Fraternity Incorporated!

Ω

So my brothers as we continue our OMEGA journey let us remember that "Friendship is Essential to the Soul." Let us all pray for traveling mercies as we adventure and make our way to Omega Chapter. As we strengthen our bonds as brothers, let us continue our commitment to Mother Omega. For those who need to be reclaimed, we need you. Omega Psi Phi is much more than just a party. It is about making a statement about this great *institution we call Omega Psi Phi Fraternity Incorporated that is 100 years old. Let the celebration begin!*

Willie Lewis

Ω

Uplift of the unknown Ques:

Ω

Long live Omega!

Ω

Long live Omega Psi Phi.

Ω

Omega Psi Phi "till the day I die."

Ω

OMEGA is a beautiful thing.

Ω

OWT: Omegas working together!

Ω

The Ques don't die -- we multiply XXXX

Ω

Que Psi Phi – 'ill the day we die!!!!

Ω

The mighty men Omega Psi Phi; long live the Psi Phi!

Ω

A Que party -- where the God's meet the Goddesses, then go to paradise.

Ω

Endeavor to present and to represent OMEGA in the most favorable and positive light possible.

Ω

We should not be seeking persons to turn into men. We should be seeking men that we can develop into Omegas!

Ω

The Ques do thy duty that is best and leave unto the Lord the rest.

Ω

Omega Psi Phi Fraternity Incorporated is a vital organization functioning effectively in every state of the union!

90

Ω

The word of the day is Uplift. As God shined his grace on us, let us shine our grace and uplift those around us. Our nation, community, and schools need our love. Seek someone out and bless them with your gifts and talents Ques.

Ω

Upon entering Omega Psi Phi Fraternity Incorporated, one of the first things I understood is that every brother that touched me had been touched by the Founding Fathers and thus passed to, and gave a transference of the power of their passions, dreams, hopes, and desires of Omega Psi Phi to me and I owe them the honor of living what they created.

Ω

I AM a Que! Although all serve their purpose, I AM a member of an organization that is the most loving, strongest, active, and brotherly! We are the warriors! We march, and even if you don't see us, know....we're heeerrrreee! Roof!

Ω

Omega Psi Phi seeks to provide opportunities, both in and outside the organization, to develop scholarship, manhood, integrity, leadership, and sound judgment; as well as the social and ethical values, which serve as a foundation in civilized societies for respectable conduct.

Ω

I AM giving all of my love....to Que Psi Phi. I will hold her up so that the Light of Omega will shine. I pray that the brothers who have passed in to Omega Chapter still smile down on her and see how all of us still work to keep her strong and virile -- all of my love, peace, and happiness....to Que Psi Phi.

Ω

Omega Psi Phi is the greatest fraternity in the World. Brothers let us continue to do our services and duty to OMEGA and continue to build the bridge as our founders of this great fraternity started back on November 17, 1911. Long live Omega Psi Phi!

Ω

In order for Omega Psi Phi to continue its path we must plant seeds amongst the youth in order to open their eyes to a new world that is foreign to them. When they see the good deeds, they will also see the brotherhood and experience the brotherhood and the mystical ways of OMEGA.

Ω

I AM proud to be a brother of Omega Psi Phi Fraternity Incorporated. While we are full of enthusiasm, charisma, humor, and diverse personalities, our main service is to help our communities, fighting injustice, become entrepreneurs, and more importantly promoting Christian Manhood, Scholarship, Perseverance, and Uplift. We will....continue to defile the odds, statistics, and stereotypes and move towards our God given purpose, roof!

Ω

It is the mission of Omega Psi Phi Fraternity Incorporated to provide a brotherhood for which men of similar ideas and backgrounds can grow and serve the local community and enrich society as a whole by implementing and supporting Omega's mandated programs and upholding her cardinal principals.

Ω

Real Omega Nobility:

The Que that performs his duty from day to day,
and perseveres through all the challenges that stand in his way.
Knowing that God has designed it so,
has located true greatness, on Mother Earth below.
The Que that serves his chapter, regardless of where,
knowing God has to have him there.
Even though the work is difficult you see,
has ascended to true Omega nobility.
For every Que there's just one test,
that each Que should give his best.
The Que who works with all the might he can
will never enter Omega Chapter owing a hu-man."

Ω

Thunder is my dog's name:

This fraternity is not for everyone.
Everyone has different views on my fraternity.
My fraternity will make you hurt, laugh, and even cry.

...Cry tears of joy if you make it to the other side.
Side by side we stand together.
Together each achieves more.
More is not what we need, quality is what we want.
Want to see it through the darkness.
Darkness is always before the light.
Light enables you to hold on when there is nothing in you.
You have choices.
Choices and decisions are very important in life.
Life is nothing but a pint of joy.
Joy comes after the blood and thunder.
Thunder is my dog's name.
Name of my fraternity is OMEGA PSI PHI.
OMEGA PSI PHI "till we die."

Ω

A toast to the men of Omega Psi Phi:

My father, who lay on his deathbed,
Said, Son one last word 'er I die.
The end is so close
that I must drink a toast.
To the men of Omega Psi Phi
To the men who stand firm
in their precepts.
To the men who stand fast
in their love.
Who live and who die
and who let the juice fly.
To the men of Omega Psi Phi.
To the men who build
dreams of the future,
to the men who dare

make them come true.
Who take time to rejoice
with the brothers of choice.
To the men of the fraternity Que.
To the men who love the fair ladies.
To the men whom the ladies rely.
Women love to recluse,
with the their flagons of juice.
And the men of Omega Psi Phi ....

Ω

I AM that Que:

I AM NOT A DOG, even though those misunderstand me would view me otherwise because I posses a DAWG-MATIC determination to make changes and the tenacity to See It Through, the loyalty of man`s best friend and the GUARDIANSHIP to protect the ones I love.

My colors are "Royal Purple" and "Old Gold". My cardinal principles are "Manhood", "Scholarship", "Perseverance", "Uplift;" therefore, I AM a combination of all these things.

I AM Royal Purple like the robe of JESUS the CHRIST, heart is noble, and my soul is that of a humble man. Royal purple is a royal color. Royal Purple is a mysterious color associated with both nobility and spirituality.

I AM Old Gold like my friendship to my brothers; it is more valuable and more enduring than South African diamonds.

I AM MANHOOD no one will be able to ride my back because my body is upright, my head is high, and my heart is strong for I fear no experience or no one but, love and respect my Lord and Savior, JESUS the CHRIST.

I AM SCHOLARSHIP as my mind is my greatest weapon and I AM a man of intuitive wit and intellect. I do not toy with idle thoughts because I AM

95

a world changer.

I AM PERSEVERNCE because I possess a strong mind and will. I AM like the everlasting love of GOD, persevering through trials and troubles long after all others have given up hope. I stay steadfast to the purpose of Omega Psi Phi Fraternity Incorporated and the cause of Uplifting humanity.

I AM UPLIFT because my spirit is free as the wind and as rich as the combined weight of the western world. We are here to help others attain a higher intellectual, moral, or Spiritual level and improve the living conditions of others.

I AM an OMEGA MAN; it is unwise to consider me otherwise.

I AM what men wish to be, and what women wish her man and sons to become.

Ω

Omega Men, A Cut Above The Rest:

Drawn from the color of royalty and sealed with the hue of the most precious metal, we, who are Omega Men, are tried and tested by the "burning sands." Those who knock and are accepted are without a doubt brothers until the day they die. Omega Men are a cut above the rest.

*Molded by the cardinal principles of Manhood, Scholarship, Perseverance, and Uplift our four Founding Fathers -- **Frank Coleman, Oscar J. Cooper, Ernest E. Just** and **Edgar A. Love**- created a fraternity that embodied all the qualities of true manhood and brotherhood. And adherence to those principles sets us apart, definitely making Omega Men a cut above the rest.*

Clothed with the armor of our brotherhood, strengthened by our manhood, affirmed by our scholarship, solidified by our perseverance and uplifted by our principles, we "move mountains" while others make excuses. That is why we are the best, a cut above the rest.

From rural areas to urban settings; from the ornate structures for worshipping God to the business "jungles" of corporate life and from the political arena to the "hills" of fellowship, Omega men have led the way, where others dare not follow. For this reason and many others, Omega Men are definitely a cut above the rest.

Our efforts to render service to our communities are tempered only by the recognition of humility in serving our Creator and fellow man. When all else fails, true Omega Men count on the greatest brotherhood in this world to be there. Omega Men know without a doubt - and make no apology - we are the best, a cut above the rest.

Ω

Am I My Brother's Keeper:

*If you were my brother's keeper
Will my best interest be at hand?
Or will you catch an attitude
when I cannot meet your demands?*

*If you were my brother's keeper
will you be there in times of need?
Or will you let our golden friendship
Be destroyed by jealousy, envy, and greed?*

*If you were my brother's keeper
would you always help me out?
Or would you take me to the green
when I didn't set it out?*

*If you were my brother's keeper
would you put me right on track?*

Lay down your life in times of need?
Would you always have my back?

If you were my brother's keeper
would you let anything come between us?
Talk to me behind my back?
Would I ever lose your trust?

If you were my brother's keeper
would you fight me over a girl?
Would you disrespect my family?
Would you divulge my secret pearl?

But I know you're my keeper
Because we have a common goal
Uplift is important and
FRIENDSHIP IS ESSENTIAL TO THE SOUL

I know you're my keeper
And our family is large and strong,
Knowledge and manhood is our infrastructure and
"Omega Dear" is our song

I know you are my keeper
And our bind is no facade
You're always willing to die for me,
And our strength comes from God

I know you're my keeper
Proud, conscientious, and bold
I know you will never leave me
Because your blood is ROYAL PURPLE and your heart is made of OLD
GOLD!

About the Author:

*Marzette Henderson Jr., famously and infamously known as Endo, was born and raised in Chicago, IL and currently resides in Chicago's south side with his wife Ayana. He graduated from Western Illinois University with a Bachelors of Science in Law Enforcement Justice Administration. The author has been called to uplift the Ques now and forever through **Omega Psi Phi Ultimate UPLIFT: 1911 to 2011 to Beyond.** He received membership through the prestigious chapter Epsilon Beta, affectionately known as Gangster EB. He likes to ride motorcycles for fun. The author also loves staying in fighting trim and uplifting the community.*

CPSIA information can be obtained
at www.ICGtesting.com
Printed in the USA
BVOW06s1019131117
500270BV00017B/64/P